W9-BBY-266

Let's create

WOOD and CORK

Gareth Stevens Publishing
A WORLD ALMANAC EDUCATION GROUP COMPANY

Please visit our web site at: www.garethstevens.com
For a free color catalog describing Gareth Stevens Publishing's
list of high-quality books and multimedia programs,
call 1-800-542-2595 (USA) or 1-800-387-3178 (Canada).
Gareth Stevens Publishing's fax: (414) 332-3567.

Library of Congress Cataloging-in-Publication Data

Wood and cork.
　　p. cm. — (Let's create!)
　Summary: Step-by-step instructions show how to use different forms of wood
or cork to create original craft projects.
　Includes bibliographical references.
　ISBN 0-8368-3749-5 (lib. bdg.)
　1. Woodwork—Juvenile literature.　2. Cork craft—Juvenile literature.
[1. Woodwork.　2. Cork craft.　3. Handicraft.] I. Series.
TT185.W6516　2003
745.51—dc21
　　　　　　　　　　　　　　　　　　　2003045407

This North American edition first published in 2003 by
Gareth Stevens Publishing
A World Almanac Education Group Company
330 West Olive Street, Suite 100
Milwaukee, WI 53212　USA

First published as *¡Vamos a crear! Madera y corcho* with an original copyright © 2001
by Parramón Ediciones, S.A., – World Rights, text and illustrations by Parramón's Editorial
Team. This U.S. edition copyright © 2004 by Gareth Stevens, Inc.　Additional end matter
copyright © 2004 by Gareth Stevens, Inc.

English Translation: Colleen Coffey
Gareth Stevens Series Editor: Dorothy L. Gibbs
Gareth Stevens Designer: Katherine A. Goedheer

All rights reserved. No part of this book may be reproduced, stored in a retrieval
system, or transmitted in any form or by any means, electronic, mechanical, photocopying,
recording, or otherwise, without the prior written permission of the copyright holder.

Printed in Spain

1 2 3 4 5 6 7 8 9 07 06 05 04 03

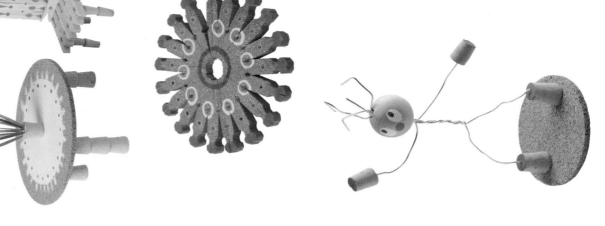

Table of Contents

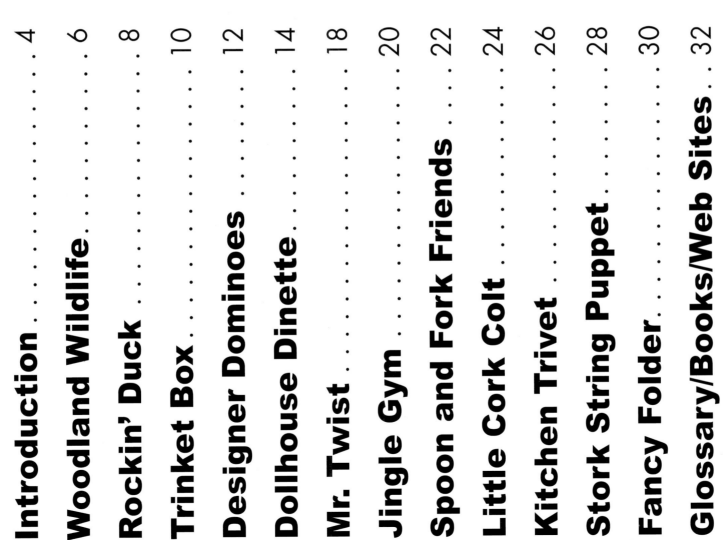

Introduction

Wood is the hardest part of a tree. Because there are many different types of trees, there are also many different types of wood. How wood looks and feels and how heavy it is depends on the type of tree it comes from. Cork, on the other hand, is a soft, spongy material. It comes from the bark of a particular type of tree — the cork oak tree.

Both wood and cork are materials commonly found around the house. We have wood furniture and wooden spoons, clothespins, and toothpicks. We also have cork bottle stoppers and cork bulletin boards. Wood and cork are used to make many different objects we use every day.

Wood and cork are also good materials for easy-to-make craft projects. Look around the house to find objects made of wood or cork, then use some of these objects to have fun making crafts.

This book offers twelve imaginative ideas for using wood and cork. You can make a nifty covered box, an original game of dominoes, a useful and decorative folder, and many other interesting items.

To make the projects in this book, you will not have to use nails, saws, or any other tools that are difficult or dangerous to operate. One or two projects call for small tools, such as wire cutters or a hand drill. Always ask a grown-up to help you use these tools.

For many of these projects, you will need thin sheets of wood or cork. You can find these materials at craft shops or at stores that specialize in wood products and even at some hardware stores.

Watch for special instructions at the end of each project to try other great ideas. Sometimes, making just one small change creates a very different result.

Now, don't you think you could have lots of fun with cork and wood?

Woodland Wildlife

With thin sheets of wood, you can bring plants and animals to life in a picturesque woodland scene.

You will need:
- colored marker
- thin sheets of wood in light and dark shades
- scissors
- white glue
- flat green toothpicks
- clip-style clothespins

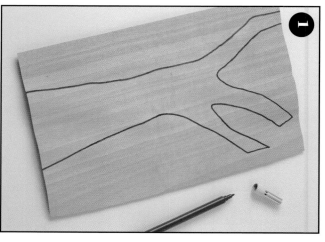

1 Use a colored marker to draw the trunk and branches of a tree on a light-colored sheet of wood.

2 Cut out the tree with scissors. Glue flat green toothpicks along the bottom of the trunk to look like grass.

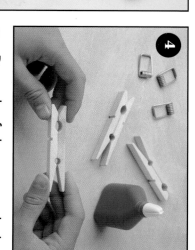

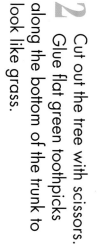

3 Draw leaf shapes on dark-colored sheets of wood. Cut out the leaves and glue them onto the tree's branches.

4 Take apart a clothespin, then glue it back together without the metal spring.

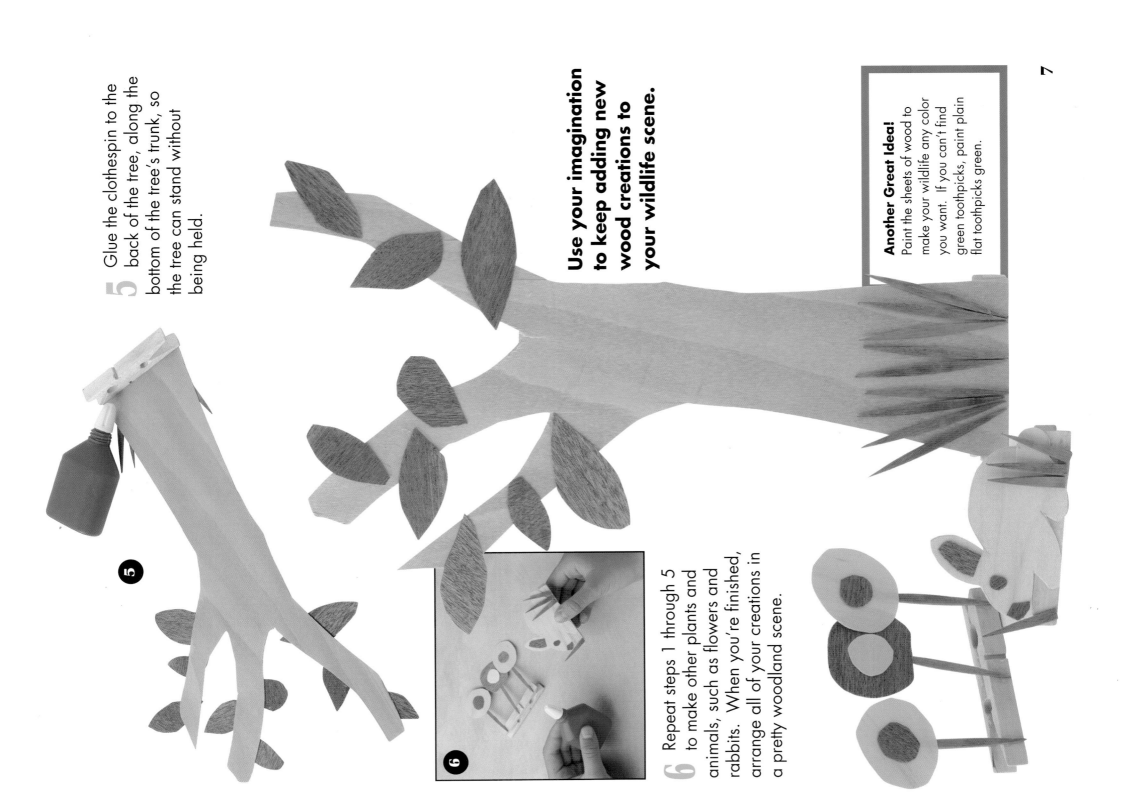

5 Glue the clothespin to the back of the tree, along the bottom of the tree's trunk, so the tree can stand without being held.

Use your imagination to keep adding new wood creations to your wildlife scene.

6 Repeat steps 1 through 5 to make other plants and animals, such as flowers and rabbits. When you're finished, arrange all of your creations in a pretty woodland scene.

Another Great Idea!
Paint the sheets of wood to make your wildlife any color you want. If you can't find green toothpicks, paint plain flat toothpicks green.

Rockin' Duck

This toy duck can really rock. All it needs is a little push. The secret is a circle of thin, lightweight cork.

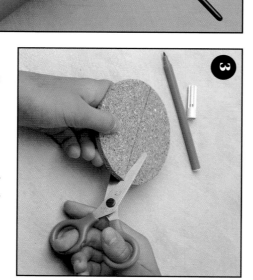

1 Use a colored marker to draw the shapes of a duck's head and tail on a sheet of thin cork. Cut out both shapes with scissors.

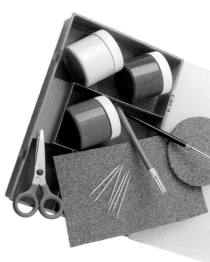

2 Paint the beak orange. Paint the eyes white and green. Paint the end of the tail white.

3 Draw a straight line across the middle of the round piece of cork. Cut along the line to make two half circles that are exactly the same size.

You will need:

- colored marker
- sheet of thin cork
- scissors
- orange, white, and green acrylic paints
- paintbrush
- round piece of thin cork, 4 inches (10 centimeters) in diameter
- round toothpicks

5 To attach the head and the tail to the two sides of the duck's body, push a toothpick through all three pieces of cork at each end of the body. Leave a small amount of space between the pieces.

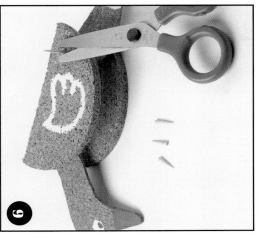

5

6 Cut off the ends of the toothpicks that are still sticking out.

Set your duck on any flat surface, then gently tap its head or tail — and watch it rock!

4 Paint a white wing in the middle of each half circle. The half circles are the two sides of the duck's body.

4

Another Great Idea!
Instead of a head and a tail, cut out a mast and a sail to make a rockin' boat.

Trinket Box

The wooden sticks from Popsicles or ice cream bars make a terrific covered box for all your tiny trinkets. Add a piece of cork to lift the lid.

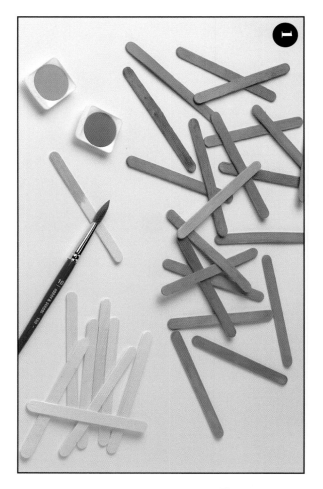

You will need:
- green and orange watercolor paints
- paintbrush
- 60 Popsicle sticks
- white glue
- large cork bottle stopper
- sharp cutting tool

1 Use watercolor paints to make 20 green Popsicle sticks and 20 orange Popsicle sticks. Leave 20 sticks unpainted.

2 To make the bottom of the box, glue the ends of 11 sticks onto two parallel orange sticks. Alternate colors as you glue the sticks in place.

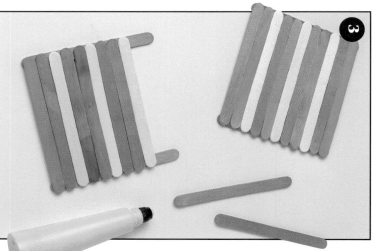

3 Repeat step 2 to make a cover for the box.

4 Glue more sticks around all four sides of the box bottom, one layer on top of another. Make eight layers, alternating the colors of the sticks for each layer.

5 Have a grown-up cut a large cork bottle stopper in half with a sharp cutting tool.

6 Glue one half of the cork stopper onto the lid of the box, in the center, to make a handle.

Your covered box is ready to fill with small objects of any kind. With its bright colors, it would make a beautiful jewelry box.

Another Great Idea!
Change the shape of the box by making the bottom and the cover a triangle, a diamond, or a hexagon.

Designer Dominoes

A sheet of cork and lots of thumbtacks, in a variety of colors, are almost everything you need to design your own dominoes. Here's how to make your next game an original.

1 On a sheet of cork, draw rectangles 2 x 4 inches (5 x 10 cm).

2 Cut out the rectangles with scissors.

You will need:

- sheet of cork, ¼ inch (6 millimeters) thick
- colored marker
- ruler
- scissors
- thin, flat strips of wood
- white glue
- white, blue, red, green, black, and orange thumbtacks

3 Cut thin strips of wood into pieces that are each 2 inches (5 cm) long.

5

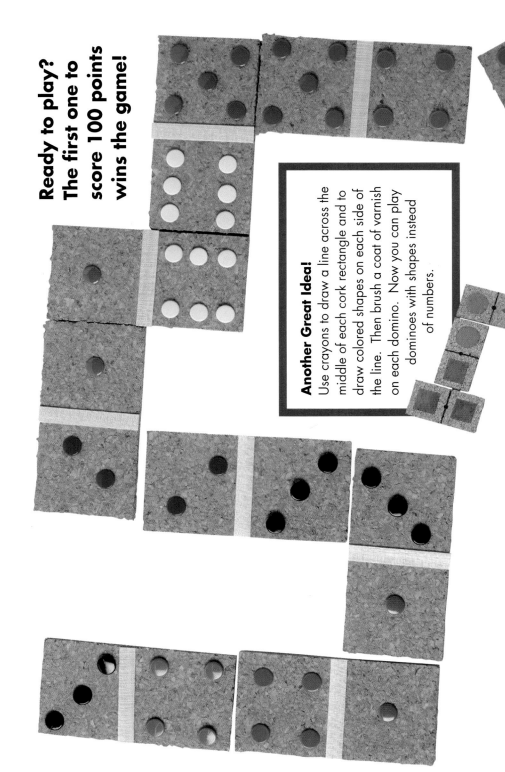

5 Push one to six colored thumbtacks into the cork rectangles on each side of the piece of wood. Use a different color for each number.

Ready to play? The first one to score 100 points wins the game!

Another Great Idea!
Use crayons to draw a line across the middle of each cork rectangle and to draw colored shapes on each side of the line. Then brush a coat of varnish on each domino. Now you can play dominoes with shapes instead of numbers.

4

4 Glue one piece of wood across the middle of each cork rectangle.

Dollhouse Dinette

Making furniture for a dollhouse takes patience and imagination as well as wood and cork.

You will need:

- clip-style clothespins
- white glue
- small cork bottle stoppers
- large cork bottle stoppers
- round piece of thin cork, 8 inches (20 cm) in diameter
- white, red, blue, and green paints
- paintbrush
- Popsicle sticks
- flat toothpicks

1 To make a chair, take apart 11 clothespins and glue them back together without the metal springs.

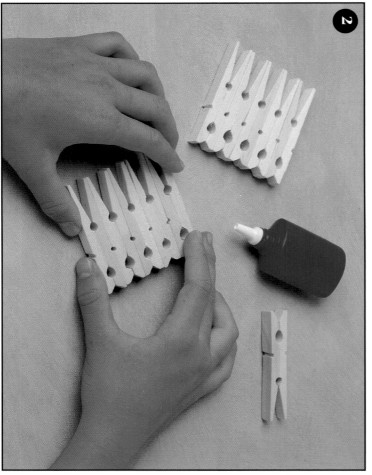

2 Glue together 5 clothespins for the back of the chair and another 5 clothespins for the seat of the chair.

3 Glue the last clothespin across the seat of the chair and glue the back on top of it.

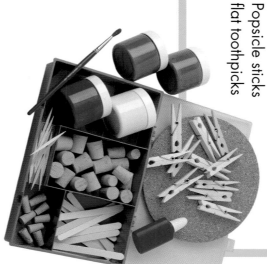

4 To make a leg for the chair, glue together 2 small cork bottle stoppers, exactly as shown in the picture. Make four legs.

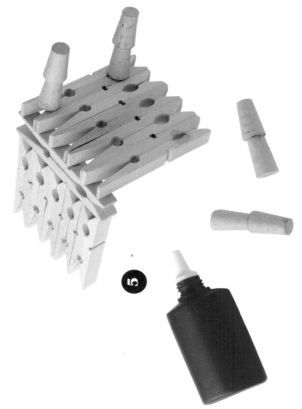

5 Glue the four legs to the bottom of the chair's seat. Glue on one leg at each corner of the seat.

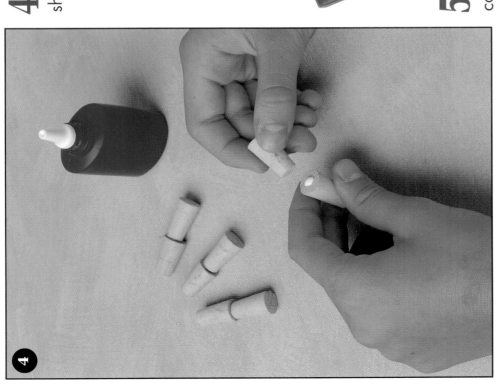

6 To make a leg for a table, glue together 3 large cork bottle stoppers, the same way you made a chair leg. Make three table legs.

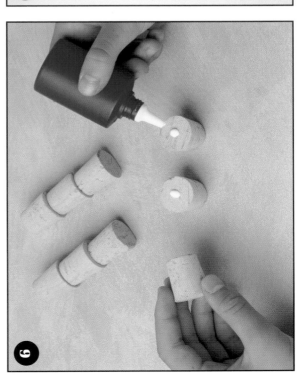

7 For the top of the table, paint a round piece of thin cork in a white and red design that looks like a tablecloth.

8 Glue the table legs onto the back side of the painted cork circle.

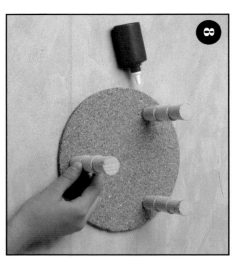

9 To make a bookshelf, paint 8 Popsicle sticks blue.

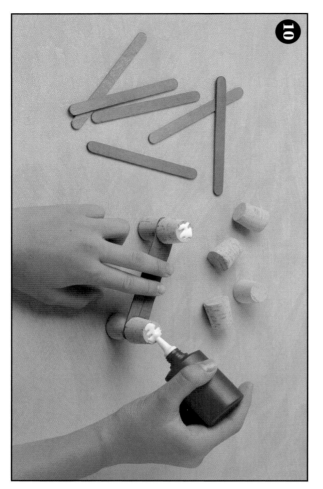

10 Glue both ends of 2 blue Popsicle sticks, laying side by side, to the narrow, flat ends of 2 large cork bottle stoppers. Then glue the wide ends of two more cork stoppers on top of the 2 sticks.

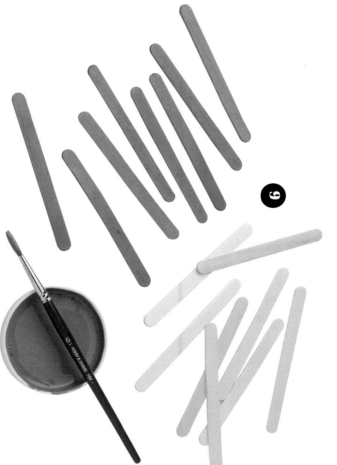

11 Repeat step 10 until you have four shelves, but do not glue cork stoppers on top of the last two sticks.

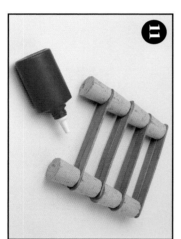

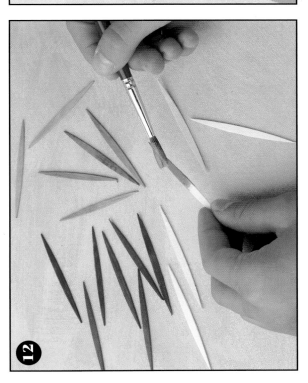

12 To make a flowerpot, paint 7 flat toothpicks green and another 7 flat toothpicks red.

13 Stick all the toothpicks into a large cork bottle stopper. Glue the stopper to the tabletop in the center of the painted tablecloth.

You have just furnished one room in your dollhouse! Use your imagination to make miniature furniture for more rooms.

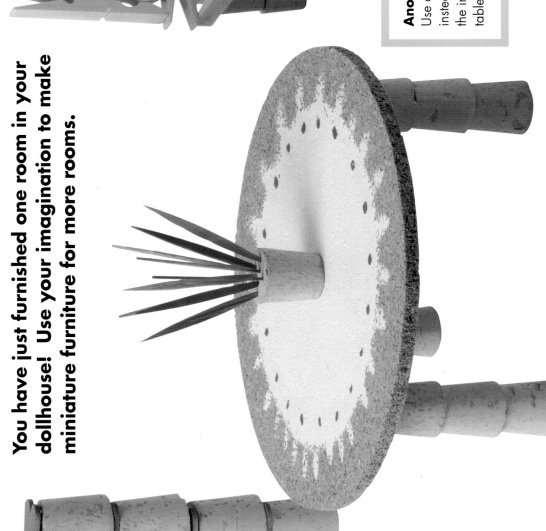

Another Great Idea!
Use a rectangle of thin cork, instead of a circle, and combine the instructions for making a table and a chair to build a bed.

Mr. Twist

What can you do with a wooden bead, a "twistful" of wire, and four corks? Make a person to pose!

You will need:

- wire cutters
- wire
- large wooden bead
- scissors
- small square of thin cork
- green, white, and orange paints
- paintbrushes
- 2 small and 2 medium cork bottle stoppers
- white glue
- round piece of cork, about 4 inches (10 cm) in diameter

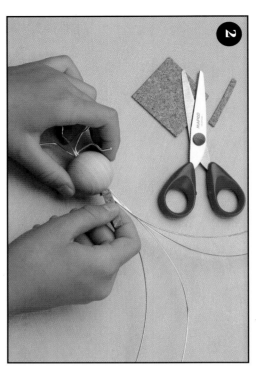

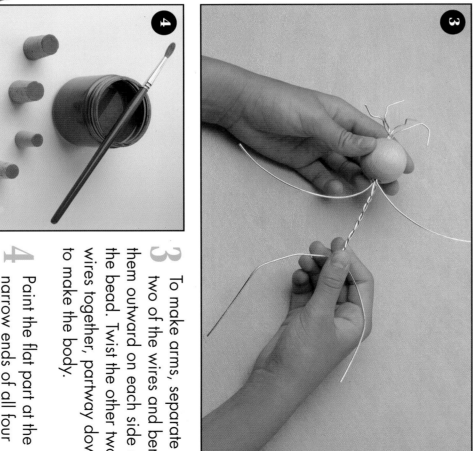

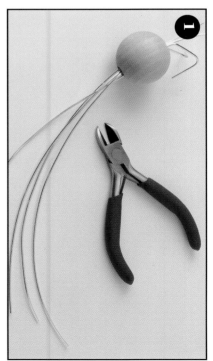

1 Cut four pieces of wire that are each 10 inches (25 cm) long. Thread all four wires through the hole in a large wooden bead. Fold over the top ends of the wires.

2 Cut small pieces of thin cork and press them lightly into the hole of the bead so the wires do not move around.

3 To make arms, separate two of the wires and bend them outward on each side of the bead. Twist the other two wires together, partway down, to make the body.

4 Paint the flat part at the narrow ends of all four cork bottle stoppers green.

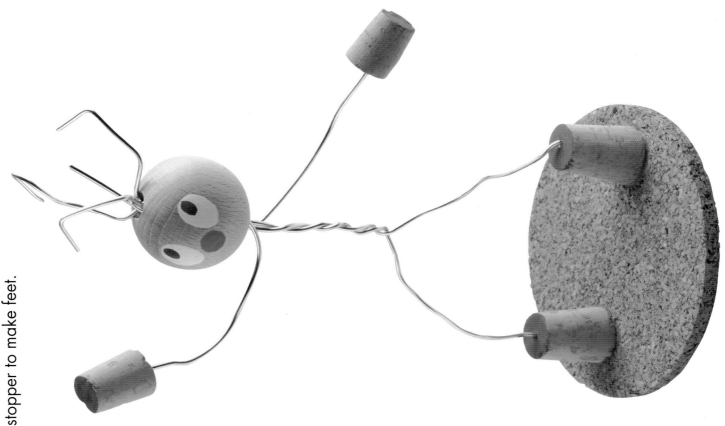

5 Stick each wire arm into the unpainted end of a small cork bottle stopper to make hands. Stick each end of the twisted wires into the painted end of a medium cork bottle stopper to make feet.

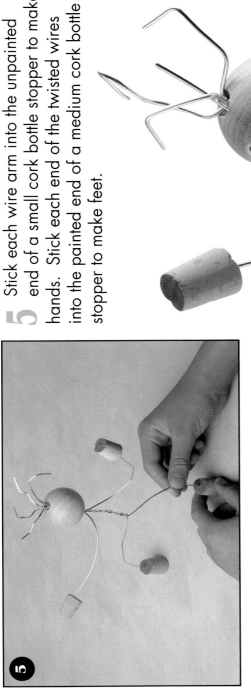

6 Glue the feet to a round piece of cork.

7 Paint a face on the wooden bead. Use white and green paints for the eyes and orange paint for the nose.

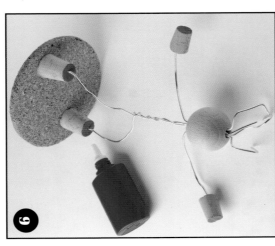

Another Great Idea!
Use more wooden beads and cork stoppers, and give the wire a new twist, to create a whole menagerie of characters.

Meet Mr. Twist! By bending his wires, you can pose him many different ways.

Jingle Gym

Use a handful of toothpicks and a couple of cork circles to create a musical instrument that looks like a gymnasium for a jingle bell.

You will need:
- colored marker
- 2 round pieces of cork, 4 inches (10 cm) in diameter
- red, blue, and yellow flat toothpicks
- large jingle bell
- glue

1 Make twenty dots with a colored marker around the edge of a round piece of cork.

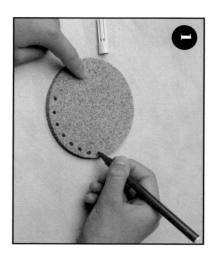

2 Stick one toothpick into every dot, alternating the three colors.

3 Place a jingle bell on the piece of cork, inside the toothpicks.

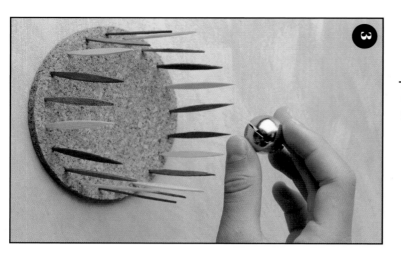

3 Rest another piece of cork on the ends of the toothpicks that are sticking out. Gently press the cork down onto the toothpicks so the ends stick in the cork. If you want to, you can use a pick to make small holes where the toothpicks should go.

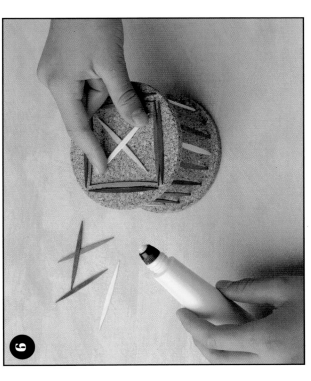

5 To decorate the outside of each cork circle, glue on red and blue toothpicks, making a square shape with each color.

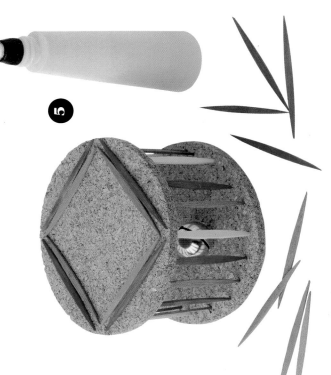

6 To finish the decoration, glue a cross made of yellow toothpicks in the center of the square.

Roll your jingle gym across the floor like a wheel to hear its delightful sound.

Another Great Idea!
Decorate your jingle gym by painting the cork or by making a flower out of colored thumbtacks on it.

Spoon and Fork Friends

A spoonful of creativity becomes a forkful of fun when you turn some simple wooden salad utensils into two finely dressed friends.

1 Paint the handle of a wooden spoon red and paint the handle of a wooden fork green. Let the paint dry.

You will need:
- red, green, white, orange, and black paints
- paintbrushes
- wooden salad spoon
- wooden salad fork
- very small cork
- bottle stoppers
- white glue

2 Use your fingertip to paint white polka dots on the handle of the spoon. Use a brush to paint wide white stripes on the handle of the fork. With a smaller brush, paint thin red stripes on top of the white stripes.

3 For hair, paint the tip of the spoon green and the teeth of the fork orange.

4 Paint faces on both the spoon and the fork. Give each face eyes, a mouth, and cheeks.

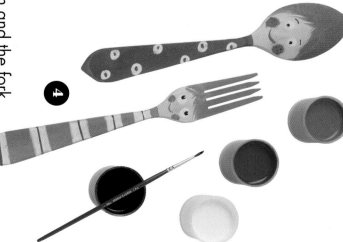

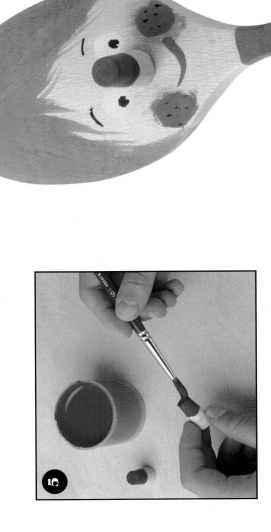

5 To make noses, paint the narrow ends of two very small cork bottle stoppers red.

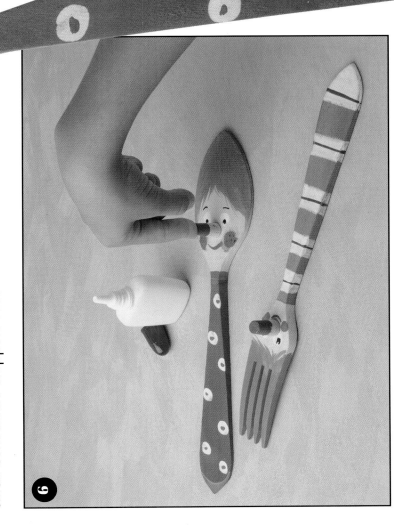

6 Glue one cork nose to the face on the spoon and glue the other cork nose to the face on the fork.

Give the decorated utensils names and make up a story about them. Use your spoon and fork friends as puppets to act out the story.

Another Great Idea!
Decorate utensils of all different sizes to create a whole family of spoon and fork friends.

Little Cork Colt

Cork bottle stoppers are very useful, not only for covering bottles but also to make awesome animal toys. Follow these simple, step-by-step instructions to make a toy horse.

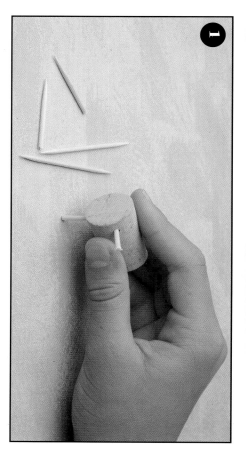

1 Cut off both ends of a toothpick and stick them, point first, into the wide end of a large cork bottle stopper. The toothpicks should be almost on opposite sides of the cork. The cork stopper is the head of the horse. The toothpicks are its ears.

2 To make the horse's neck and body, stick one end of a toothpick into the wide end of the head. Then stick the other end of the same toothpick into the narrow end of another large cork stopper.

3 Cut one end off of a toothpick and stick it into the wide, flat end of the horse's body. Stick a small cork stopper on the other end of the toothpick to form a tail.

4 For legs and hooves, stick 4 toothpicks into the narrow ends of 4 small cork stoppers. Then stick the legs into the body.

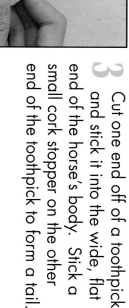

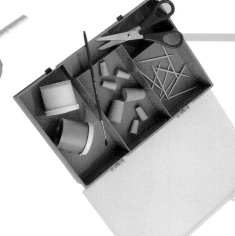

You will need:
- scissors
- round toothpicks
- large cork bottle stoppers
- small cork bottle stoppers
- white and green paints
- paintbrush

Making toy horses is so easy that you'll be able to make a whole herd in two shakes of a colt's tail.

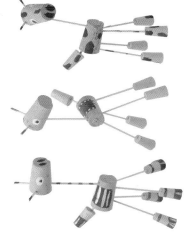

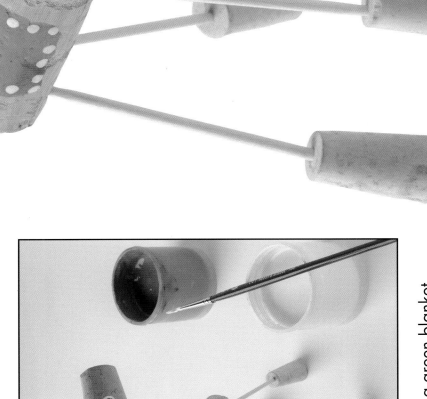

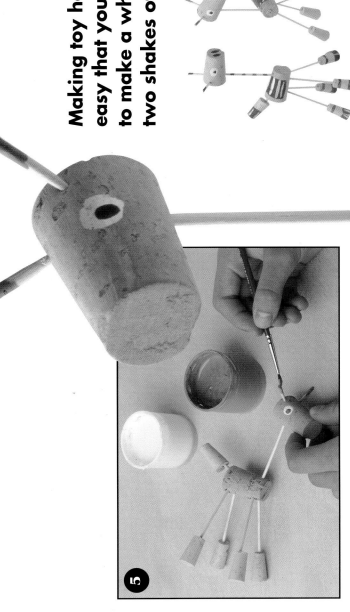

5 Paint a face on the horse's head. Paint the eyes white and green and paint the tips of the ears green.

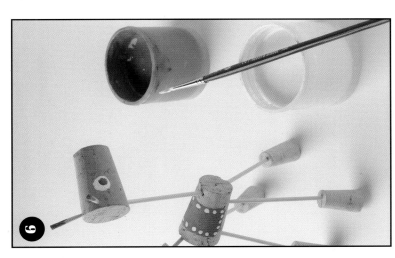

6 Paint a green blanket on the horse's body and decorate it by painting white dots around the edges.

Another Great Idea!
Stick a thumbtack into the bottom of each hoof so your colt will make clip-clop sounds as it trots.

Kitchen Trivet

When should you bring wooden clothespins to the dinner table? When you have made a useful and decorative trivet out of them, of course!

You will need:

- clip-style clothespins
- white glue
- red, green, and white paints
- paintbrushes
- toothbrush

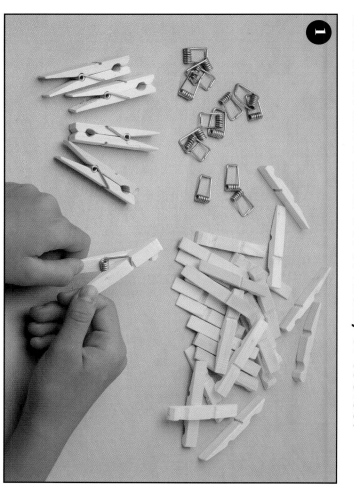

1 Take apart 19 clothespins and remove the metal spring that holds each clothespin together.

2 With the flat sides facing each other, glue together the two wooden parts of each clothespin.

3 After the glue on each clothespin has dried, glue together the pointed ends of all of the clothespins to form a circle.

5 Decorate the top of the trivet by painting a design of green and white circles around holes in the clothespins. Paint a big red circle around the large hole in the center of the trivet.

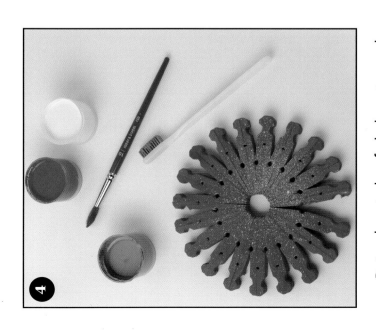

4 Paint the circle of clothespins red, on both sides. When the red paint is dry, spatter green and white paints over it with a toothbrush.

Now your pretty trivet is ready to protect the dinner table from any hot pot, pan, or plate you care to place on it.

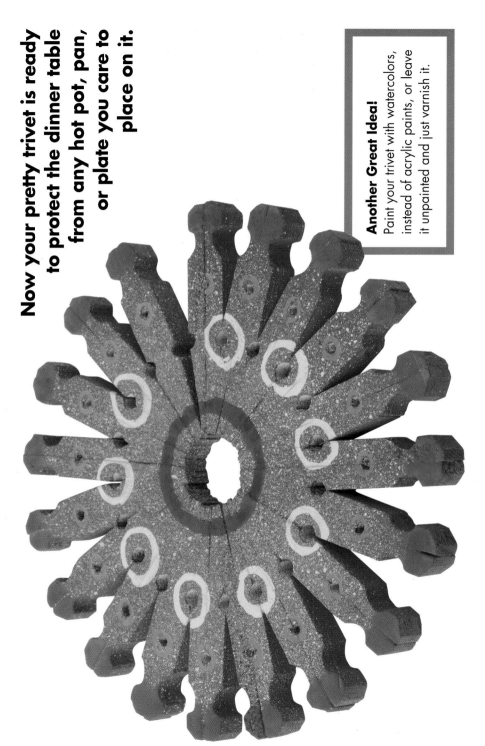

Another Great Idea!
Paint your trivet with watercolors, instead of acrylic paints, or leave it unpainted and just varnish it.

Stork String Puppet

A cork stork held together with string can't fly — but you can make it dance!

1 Stick 2 green thumbtacks into a medium cork ball, for eyes, and use a black marker to draw in the pupils.

You will need:

- green and brown thumbtacks
- medium cork balls
- black permanent marker
- flat toothpicks
- red, green, and orange watercolor paints
- paintbrush
- small cork balls
- scissors
- brown string
- ruler
- clip-style clothespins
- white glue

2 To make a beak, paint a toothpick red and stick it into the cork ball between the thumbtack eyes.

3 Paint 3 toothpicks green and stick them into another medium cork ball. The green toothpicks are tail feathers.

4 Paint 6 toothpicks orange and stick them into two small cork balls to make feet. Put 3 toothpicks in each ball.

5 Cut brown string into two 8-inch (20-cm) pieces, two 6-inch (15-cm) pieces, and a 4-inch (10-cm) piece.

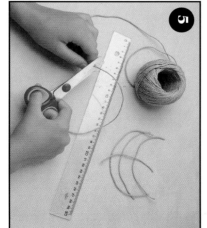

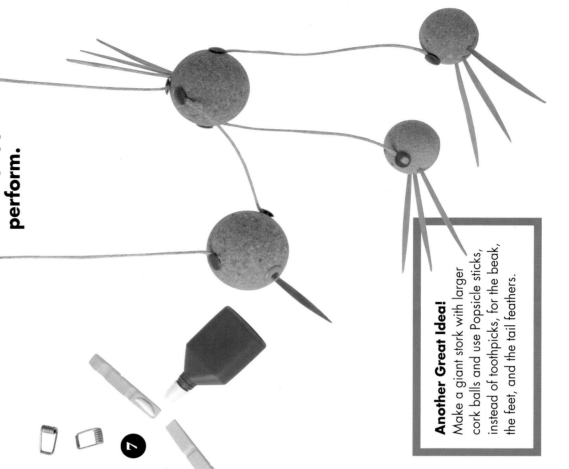

Just wiggle its strings to make your stork puppet perform.

6 Use brown thumbtacks to attach the pieces of string to the cork balls. Attach one of the 8-inch (20-cm) pieces to the head and the other one to the body. The 6-inch strings are the legs. The 4-inch string is the neck.

7 Take apart 2 clothespins and remove the metal springs. Glue the sides of each clothespin together end to end. Then glue these two long pieces together in the form of a cross.

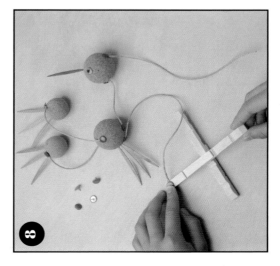

8 Use 2 green thumbtacks to attach the strings coming from the stork's head and body to two ends of the wooden cross.

Another Great Idea!
Make a giant stork with larger cork balls and use Popsicle sticks, instead of toothpicks, for the beak, the feet, and the tail feathers.

Fancy Folder

This folder is fabulous! It is beautifully decorated but also very, very strong. Made of wood, it could last a lifetime.

You will need:

- colored marker
- ruler
- 2 rectangles of thin wood, 13 x 10 inches (33 x 25 cm)
- hand drill
- orange and fuchsia paints
- paintbrushes
- scissors
- black elastic cord

1 Use a colored marker to make dots, 1 inch (2.5 cm) apart, along one long side of a rectangular piece of thin wood. Have a grown-up help you use a hand drill to make a hole where each dot is.

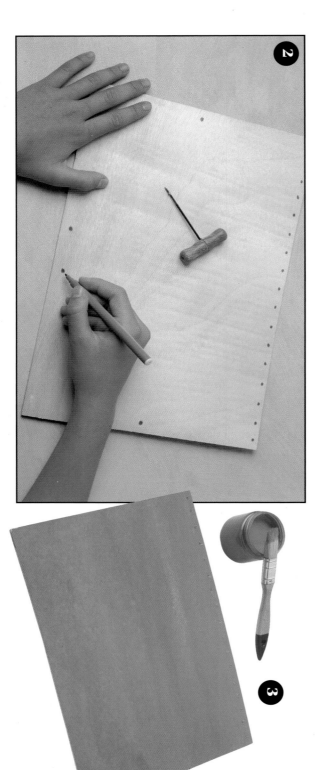

2 Repeat step 1 on another piece of wood, then mark and drill one hole in the middle of each short side and two holes, 2 inches (5 cm) apart, in the middle of the other long side.

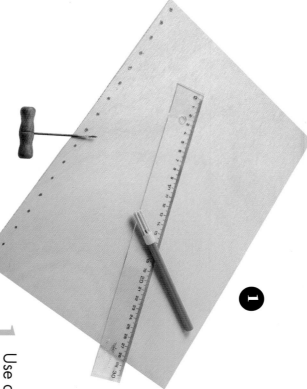

3 For the cover of the folder, paint one side of the first piece of wood orange.

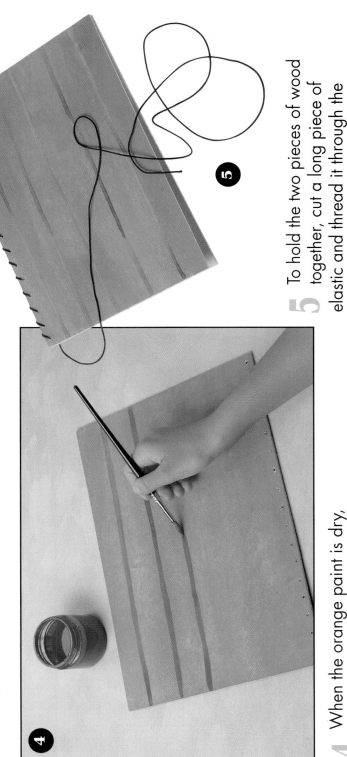

4 When the orange paint is dry, paint fuchsia stripes across it.

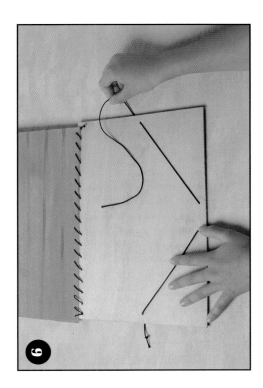

5 To hold the two pieces of wood together, cut a long piece of elastic and thread it through the holes on the sides with lots of holes.

6 Thread another piece of elastic through the holes at the top and on the sides of the back of the folder. Tie a knot at each end of the elastic to keep it from coming out of the holes. Stretch this piece of elastic over the front of the folder to keep it closed.

Carry your favorite drawings in this fancy folder, which just happens to be another one of your creations.

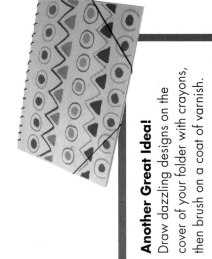

Another Great Idea!
Draw dazzling designs on the cover of your folder with crayons, then brush on a coat of varnish.

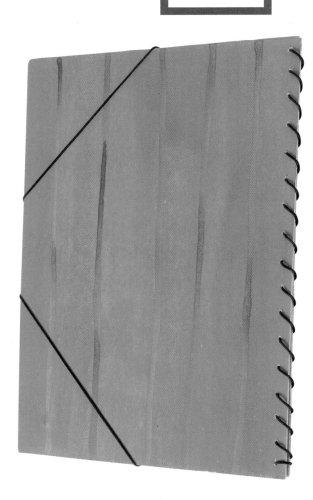

Glossary

alternate: (v) to arrange something in a repeating pattern

colt: a young male horse

designer: introduced and accepted as a new style or a change of style

hexagon: a shape that has six sides

menagerie: a collection of different kinds of animals, usually in cages

miniature: a small model of an object that is normally much larger

parallel: side by side, the same distance apart at all points, and never touching

picturesque: like a work of art

pose: (v) to move the parts of the body into particular positions

shades: the same color appearing lighter and darker

spatter: to scatter or sprinkle, forming a spotted pattern; to splatter

trinket: a small, decorative object

trivet: a small platform placed under a hot serving dish to keep the surface of a table from being damaged

utensils: tools used for cooking or eating

More Books to Read

Clothespin Crafts. Margaret Holtschlag and Carol Trojanowski (Random House)

Craft Stick Mania. Christine M. Irvin (Children's Press)

Easy Carpentry Projects for Children. Jerome Edward Leavitt (Dover Publications)

A Kid's Guide to Crafts: Wood Projects. Tim Bramlett (Stackpole Books)

Look What You Can Make With Craft Sticks. Kelly Milner Halls, ed. (Boyds Mills Press)

Terrific Toys. Handy Crafts (series). Gillian Souter (Gareth Stevens)

Web Sites

Projects for Craft Sticks and Woodsies. www.makingfriends.com/craftsticks.htm

Twig Crafts. www.enchantedlearning.com/crafts/twigs